DOLLS OF THE INDIANS

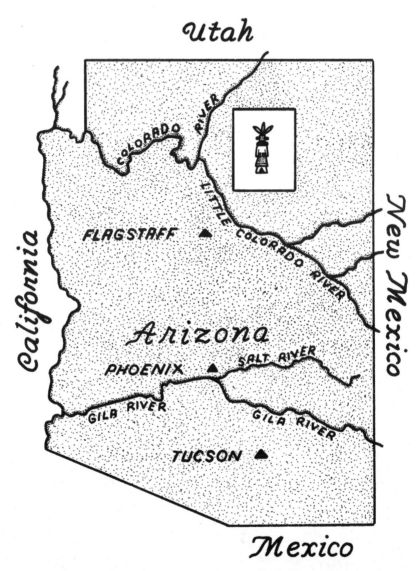

THE WHITE BLOCK SHOWN ON THE MAP ABOVE
INDICATES THE LOCATION OF THE HOPI INDIAN
RESERVATION.

DOLLS
Of The
INDIANS

By
Elsie V. Hanauer

**South Brunswick and New York:
A. S. Barnes and Company
London: Thomas Yoseloff Ltd**

A. S. Barnes and Company, Inc.
Cranbury, New Jersey 08512

Thomas Yoseloff Ltd
108 New Bond Street
London W1Y OQX, England

SBN 498 07536 2
Printed in the United States of America

CONTENTS

 Introduction

IN THE HARSH AND SEMI-ARID COUNTRY OF
NORTH EASTERN ARIZONA, THE HOPI INDIANS
CONTINUE TO LIVE IN MUCH THE SAME WAY
AS DID THEIR ANCESTORS. FROM THEIR
ANCIENT PAST, WHICH DATES BACK TO
THE 15TH CENTURY, THE HOPI HAVE RETAINED
MANY RELIGIOUS CEREMONIES. THEY BELIEVE
THAT ALL NATURE IS CONTROLLED BY THEIR
ELABORATE CEREMONIES WHICH ARE HELD
TO PLEASE THE GODS.

THE HOPI PEOPLE ARE FIRM BELIEVERS
THAT NOTHING IS LEFT TO FATE BECAUSE
FROM THEIR BIRTH THERE ARE RITES
AND CEREMONIES DESIGNED TO HELP
THEM THROUGH EVERY CRISIS OF LIFE.

Deer Kachina Mask

Kachina Spirits

MOST PROMINENT AMONG THE RELIGIOUS
OBSERVANCES OF THE HOPI ARE THEIR
CEREMONIES ASSOCIATED WITH THE
KACHINA. A KACHINA, MEANING SPIRIT-FATHER,
IS A SUPERNATURAL BEING WHO REPRESENTS
THE POWER OF AN ANCESTRAL SPIRIT WHO
IS CAPABLE OF ACTING FOR GOOD OR EVIL.

THE KACHINA SPIRITS VISIT THE HOPI VILLAGES
DURING THE FIRST HALF OF EVERY YEAR TO
BRING GIFTS AND DANCE FOR RAIN.

THERE ARE OVER 200 DIFFERENT KACHINAS,
EACH HAVING ITS OWN NAME, SPIRITUAL
CHARACTER AND SPECIFIC COSTUME. SOME
KACHINAS APPEAR EVERY YEAR, WHILE
OTHERS ARE RARELY SEEN. THIS IS BECAUSE
SOME ARE DROPPED AND NEW ONES ARE
ADDED FROM TIME TO TIME.

IT IS IMPORTANT TO REALIZE THAT KACHINAS
ARE NOT WORSHIPPED, BUT ARE LOOKED UPON
AS FRIENDS. YET NOT ALL ARE BENEVOLENT,
SOME ARE WHIPPERS WHO PUNISH OFFENDERS
OF LAWS.

Tungwup Kachina Costume

Kachina Ceremonies

THE KACHINA SPIRITS ARE BELIEVED TO LIVE IN
THE MOUNTAINS LOCATED NORTH OF FLAGSTAFF,
ARIZONA. HERE THEY SLEEP DURING THE WARM
SEASON, UNTIL AT THE TIME OF THE WINTER
SOLSTICE IN DECEMBER, THEY VISIT THE HOPI
VILLAGES. THE PURPOSE OF THEIR VISIT EVERY
YEAR IS TO BRING THE RAINS THAT HELP THE
CROPS GROW.

DURING THE KACHINA SEASON, WHICH LASTS
FROM DECEMBER TO JULY, THERE ARE FIVE
MAJOR CEREMONIES: 1. THE SOYALUNA IN
DECEMBER, 2. THE PAMURI IN JANUARY, 3. THE
POWAMU IN FEBRUARY, 4. THE PALOLOKONTI
IN MARCH AND 5. THE NIMA IN JULY WHICH
CELEBRATES THE KACHINAS DEPARTURE.

AS A RULE THE KACHINAS APPEAR IN GROUPS
OF 15 TO 30. THE PERFORMERS, ALL MASKED
AND DRESSED ALIKE, DANCE AND SING IN
UNISON. THE BASIC DANCE STEP IS STAMPING
THE GROUND WITH THE FOOT IN RHYTHM
WITH THE MUSIC. THE SONGS ARE SOMETIMES
COMPOSED FOR EACH DANCE, BUT ALL PROVE
TO USE THE SAME IDEAS AND PHRASES TO
EXPRESS THE DESIRE FOR RAIN AND GOOD CROPS.

Symbols Used On Masks

BIRD TRACK

MOON

FRIENDSHIP

CLOUDS

STAR

WARRIOR

CLOUDS

CORN

BLOSSOM

CACTUS BLOSSOM

BLOSSOM

LIGHTNING

RAINBOW

RAINBOW

SUN

12

Kachina Colors And Designs

COLORS ABOUND IN THE HOPI COUNTRY OF
SAND AND LIMITLESS SKY. WITH CONSTANT
WONDERS OF NATURE ABOVE AND AROUND
HIM, THE HOPI BEGAN TO RELATE THE COLOR
HE SAW TO CERTAIN PHASES OF HIS LIFE.
FROM THE ASSOCIATIONS GREW SYMBOLISM
IN WHICH COLOR REPRESENTS IDEAS AND
OBJECTS. COLOR IS RELATED TO DIRECTION:
NORTH IS YELLOW BECAUSE A YELLOW SKY
BRINGS WINTER STORMS. EAST IS WHITE FOR
IT SUGGESTS THE RISING SUN. THE SOUTH IS
RED BECAUSE OF THE WARM SUMMERS AND
BLUE IS WEST AS IT SUGGESTS THE PACIFIC.
THE COLOR GREEN SUGGESTS LIFE AND
FECUNDITY, WHILE BLUE-GREEN IS USUALLY
ASSOCIATED WITH THE SKY. THE UNDERWORLD
OR BELOW IS SUGGESTED WITH BLACK.

THE DECORATIVE DESIGNS PAINTED ON THE
KACHINA MASK USUALLY HAVE DEFINITE
SYMBOLIC RELATION TO THE CHARACTERIZATION.
THESE PAINTED FORMS HAVE THEIR ORIGIN IN
THE HOPI'S DEPENDENCE ON RAIN AND SUNSHINE
FOR THE MATURITY OF VEGETATION.

Mountain Sheep Kachina

Mountain Sheep Kachina

THE MOUNTAIN SHEEP MASK SHOWN
FEATURES LARGE CURVED HORNS
WHICH CARRY SYMBOLS OF CLOUDS,
RAIN AND LIGHTNING. THE FACE
OF THE BLACK MASK IS PAINTED
BLUE AND OUTLINED IN RED. A
LONG, FLAT BLACK SNOUT PROJECTS
IN THE FRONT AND SQUASH TYPE
BLOSSOM ORNAMENTS FROM
THE SIDES. A RUFF OF GREEN
FIR HIDES THE JUNCTION BETWEEN
THE MASK AND BODY.

Rugan

THE BLACK AND
GREEN MASK HAS
A RED, YELLOW
AND WHITE DESIGN
UNDER EACH EYE,
WHITE EAR TABS
AND A PROJECTING
YELLOW SNOUT.

Ho-te

THE BRIGHT YELLOW
MASK IS INTERRUPTED
BY BLACK AND RED
STARS. LARGE RED
EAR TABS AND A
BLACK SNOUT PROJECT
FROM THE MASK.

Kau-a

THE GREEN MASK IS
INTERRUPTED BY
STRIPES OF BLACK,
RED AND YELLOW.
IT HAS SLOT EYES
AND A PROJECTING
ROUND SNOUT.

Rugan

THE RUGAN KACHINA WEARS A
JUNIPER RUFF, KILT, SASH AND
GREEN MOCCASINS. HE CARRIES
A JUNIPER BRANCH IN HIS
RIGHT HAND AND A RATTLE IN
HIS LEFT.

Ho-te

THE HO-TE KACHINA USUALLY
WEARS A FIR RUFF, KILT, SASH,
FOX SKIN AND RED MOCCASINS.
HIS BODY IS PAINTED RED WITH
YELLOW SHOULDERS. HO-TE
CARRIES A BOW AND RATTLE.

Kau-a

THE KAU-A KACHINA WEARS A
FIR RUFF AND HIS BODY IS
PAINTED RED WITH YELLOW
SHOULDERS, FOREARMS AND
LEGS.

Hand →

THE BLACK MASK HAS A WHITE HAND PRINT, OUTLINED IN RED, PAINTED ON THE FRONT. LARGE RED EAR TABS PROJECT FROM THE SIDES.

← Sun Turkey

THE FACE OF THE BLUE MASK IS WHITE, OUTLINED IN RED. PROJECTING BEAK IS BLACK.

Tuhavi →

THE BLACK MASK HAS POP EYES, PROJECTING SNOUT AND WHITE HORNS.

Hand

THE HAND KACHINA WEARS A
FOX SKIN RUFF, KILT, SASH AND
RED MOCCASINS. HIS BODY IS
OFTEN PAINTED WHITE AND
HE CARRIES A RATTLE.

Sun Turkey

THE SUN TURKEY KACHINA
WEARS THE USUAL KACHINA
COSTUME. HIS BODY IS PAINTED
RED WITH BLUE AND YELLOW
SHOULDERS.

Tuhavi

THE TUHAVI KACHINA WEARS A
FOX SKIN RUFF, BREECH CLOUT,
FOX SKIN AND RED MOCCASINS.
HIS BODY IS PAINTED BLACK
WITH WHITE WARRIOR TRACKS.

Badger

THE BADGER MASK
HAS ONE SIDE PAINTED
GREEN AND THE OTHER
PINK. THE CENTER IS
WHITE AND THE SLOT
EYES ARE A YELLOW-
GREEN.

Tuskiapaya

THE TUSKIAPAYA
MASK IS BLUE
WITH LARGE RED
EAR TABS.

Kwivi

THE KWIVI MASK
IS EITHER WHITE
OR PINK AND HAS
A GREEN STEPPED
DESIGN UNDER
EACH OF THE EYES.

Badger

THE BADGER KACHINA WEARS A
FIR RUFF, KILT, SASH, FOX SKIN
AND RED MOCCASINS. A
MAIDEN'S SHAWL IS WORN
OVER THE SHOULDERS. THE
BADGER CARRIES A RATTLE.

Tuskiapaya

THE TUSKIAPAYA KACHINA
WEARS A KILT AND COLORFUL
SASH. HIS BODY IS PAINTED
RED WITH YELLOW SHOULDERS.

Kwivi

THE KWIVI KACHINA WEARS A
DOUGLAS FIR RUFF, BRIGHT
COLORED KILT, FOX SKIN AND
NO SASH. HIS BODY IS PAINTED
WHITE. HE CARRIES A RATTLE.

Kachina Impersonator

 # Kachina Impersonators

WHEN A HOPI IMPERSONATES A KACHINA BY
WEARING THE MASK AND COSTUME HE BELIEVES
THAT THE KACHINA SPIRIT ENTERS HIS BODY
AND HE BECOMES THE KACHINA THAT HE IS
IMPERSONATING.

THE MASK, MADE OF LEATHER, STRETCHED
OVER A WILLOW FRAME, IS THE UNIQUE FEATURE
OF THE IMPERSONATION. DETAILS OF THE MASK
ARE VARIED. SOME HAVE HORNS, EARS AND
SNOUTS. THE EYES ARE SOMETIMES PAINTED
IN ROUND OR RECTANGULAR FORM WHILE
SOME ARE CARVED OUT OF WOOD TO EXTEND
BEYOND THE MASK LIKE POP-EYES. THE MOUTH
MAY BE PAINTED AS A SQUARE, CIRCLE OR
TRIANGLE. IMPORTANT PAINTINGS OF CLOUDS,
LIGHTNING, STARS AND OTHER SYMBOLS OFTEN
OCCUR ON THE MASK CHEEKS. AROUND THE
LOWER EDGE OF THE MASK A COLLAR OR RUFF
OF EVERGREEN IS WORN.

THE KACHINA COSTUMES VARY, BUT THE MOST
COMMON TYPE CONSIST OF THEIR OWN WOVEN

Impersonators Cont.

COTTON PIECES: THE WHITE KILT, SASH, BELT AND A FOX SKIN ATTACHED TO THE BACK OF THE WAIST. PIECES OF GREENBOUGH ARE OFTEN TUCKED IN ARMBANDS AND LONG YARN TIES ARE FASTENED AT THE WRISTS, KNEES AND ANKLES. THE BRACELETS AND NECKLACES WORN USUALLY HAVE SOME CEREMONIAL SIGNIFICANCE. MOST ALL THE KACHINAS CARRY RATTLES OR BOW AND ARROWS IN THEIR HANDS.

Kachina Education

IT IS DURING THE COLORFUL KACHINA CEREMONIES THAT KACHINA PERFORMERS PRESENT THE CARVED WOODEN DOLLS TO THE HOPI CHILDREN. THE DOLL IS NOT JUST A TOY, BUT IS A PART OF THE RELIGIOUS EDUCATION OF THE CHILDREN. THE DOLL TEACHES KACHINA RECOGNITION AND ACTS AS A CONSTANT REMINDER OF KACHINA IMPORTANCE.

HOPI DOLL MAKER

 Kachina Dolls

KACHINA DOLLS ARE CARVED BY HOPI MEN FROM THE ROOT OF A COTTONWOOD TREE. THE WOOD IS GATHERED UP AS SUN-DRIED DRIFTWOOD USUALLY FOUND IN THE DRY WASHES. THE COTTONWOOD ROOT IS LIGHT IN WEIGHT AND CARVES QUITE EASILY. IN MANY RESPECTS IT IS SIMILIAR TO THE BALSA WOOD USED IN BUILDING MODELS.

THE FIGURE IS FIRST ROUGHED OUT WITH A POCKET KNIFE AND RASP. ONCE A DESIRED SHAPE IS ACHIEVED, THE FIGURE IS THEN RUBBED SMOOTH WITH A PIECE OF SAND-STONE. THE ARMS ARE THEN CARVED TO THE RIGHT SIZE FROM A SEPARATE PIECE OF WOOD.

THE ARMS AND OTHER ADDITIONS, SUCH AS EARS AND SNOUT ARE THEN ATTACHED TO THE DOLL WITH TINY SLIVERS OF WOOD. THEN THE ENTIRE DOLL IS COVERED WITH A COATING OF WHITE CLAY.

THE DOLL IS THEN
CAREFULLY PAINTED
AS ACCURATELY AS
POSSIBLE IN COPY
OF THE ORIGINAL
DANCER. IN MOST
CASES COMMERCIAL
POSTER PAINTS ARE
BEING USED IN
PLACE OF EARTH
PIGMENTS THAT
WERE USED IN THE
PAST.

THE FINAL TOUCHES
ARE NOW ADDED. A
RATTLE AND BOW ARE
PLACED IN THE DOLL'S
HANDS. FEATHERS,
BITS OF CLOTH AND
FUR ARE SOMETIMES
ADDED TO THE HEAD
AND BODY. IN SOME
CASES EVEN FRESH
GREENBOUGH IS
USED IN THE FINAL
DECORATION.

Cactus

Shopping For Kachinas

AT ONE TIME KACHINA DOLLS COULD BE HAD
ONLY IN HOPI VILLAGES OR FROM TRADERS.
NOW THEY ARE MADE FOR THE TOURIST TRADE
AND SELL IN SHOPS THROUGHOUT THE WEST.

THE DOLLS USUALLY RANGE IN SIZE FROM
FOUR INCHES TO AS MUCH AS TWO FEET IN
HEIGHT. THE DOLL SHOWN ON PAGE 31 ILL-
USTRATES A TYPE THAT IS TURNED ON A
LATHE RATHER THAN HANDCARVED. THESE
ARE USUALLY SMALL IN SIZE AND LOW PRICED.
THE ACTION TYPE KACHINA AS SHOWN ON
PAGE 123 AND 125, ARE BECOMING POPULAR
WITH COLLECTORS. BUT THE MAJORITY OF
DOLLS TEND TO STAND IN STIFF POSES
LIKE THOSE ILLUSTRATED ON PAGES 35
THROUGH 121.

 SINCE KACHINA DOLLS ARE A HAND-MADE
ITEM, PRICES WILL VARY WITH THE SIZE,
COMPLEXITY AND QUALITY OF CRAFTSMAN-
SHIP.

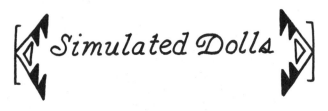

Simulated Dolls

SHOWN OPPOSITE IS A TYPE OF KACHINA DOLL FOUND ON THE MARKET THAT IS NOT CARVED BY HAND, BUT TURNED ON A LATHE. TO AUTHENTICATE THEM AS BEING INDIAN MADE, MANY ARE PAINTED BY INDIAN CRAFTSMEN. THESE MACHINE MADE DOLLS ARE USUALLY SMALL IN SIZE AND LOW PRICED. THE SIMULATED DOLLS, WHICH ARE NOT TRUE REPRE-SENTATIONS OF PARTICULAR KACHINAS, ARE EASILY RECOGNIZED BY THE TEEPEE-SHAPED NOTCH IN THE FRONT OF THE SOLID BASE. ONLY GENUINE HAND-CARVED KACHINA DOLLS HAVE INDIVIDUALLY CARVED FEET.

FOR ASSURANCE OF AUTHEN-TICITY, THE PROSPECTIVE BUYER OF KACHINA DOLLS SHOULD VISIT THE HOPI RESERVATION OR A REPUTABLE INDIAN ART DEALER.

Kachina Mother

SAID TO BE THE MOTHER OF ALL THE
KACHINAS, THIS SIMPLE SLAB FORM
DOLL IS THE TYPE GIVEN TO THE
HOPI INFANTS. BELIEVED TO BE
SIMILIAR TO DOLLS CARVED IN
PREHISTORIC DAYS THE FLAT
DOLL IS USUALLY PAINTED WHITE
WITH A BLUE AND GREEN VEST
LOOKING PATTERN. BOLD RED
STRIPES INTERRUPT THE LOWER
PORTION.

THE MOTHER KACHINA IS OFTEN A
PRINCIPAL ACTOR IN THE WATER
SERPENT CEREMONY AND MAY
ALSO APPEAR IN OTHER HOPI
CEREMONIES.

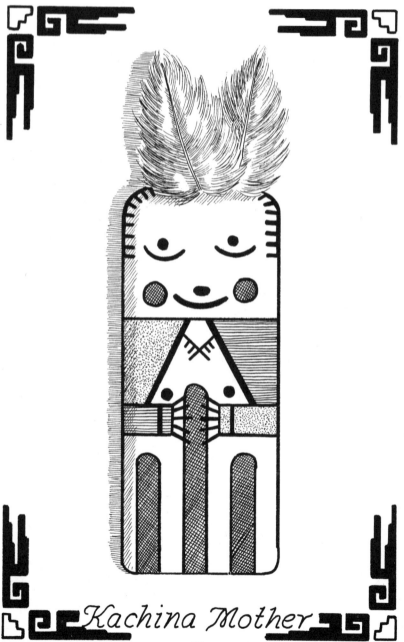

Kachina Mother

The Eagle

THE EAGLE KACHINA IS STYLIZED
REALISM WITH ITS TURQUOISE
MASK THAT HAS LARGE PROJECTING
RED TAB EARS, ROUND BLACK
EYES AND HOOKED BEAK. THE
BLACK BODY IS INTERRUPTED
BY A VEST SHAPED PATCH OF
YELLOW ON THE CHEST. THE LOWER
ARMS AND LEGS ARE ALSO BRIGHT
YELLOW TO SIMULATE THE TALONS
OF AN EAGLE. A FAN SHAPED TAIL
OF EAGLE FEATHERS IS ATTACHED
TO THE BACK AND WINGS MADE OF
EAGLE FEATHERS COVER THE ARMS.

CONNECTED WITH MEDICINE AND
CURING, THE EAGLE KACHINA
SOMETIMES APPEARS AT NIGHT
CEREMONIES IN MARCH.

The Eagle

Hemis

THE OUTSTANDING FEATURE OF
THE HEMIS KACHINA IS HIS
ELABORATE TABLETA. THE COLOR-
FUL TABLETA IS USUALLY BLUE,
OUTLINED IN RED AND PAINTED
WITH PHALLIC AND CLOUD SYMBOLS.
THE CASE MASK IS PAINTED HALF
BLUE AND HALF WHITE OR RED.
THE HEMIS WEARS A GREEN FIR
RUFF, WHITE KILT, SASH AND A FOX
SKIN. A HANK OF BLUE YARN IS
WORN ACROSS HIS BLACK CHEST
WHICH IS INTERRUPTED BY WHITE
HALF MOON DESIGNS. THE HEMIS
SOMETIMES CARRIES A RATTLE
AND SPRIG OF DOUGLAS FIR.

THE HEMIS KACHINA IS USUALLY
THE PRINCIPAL CHARACTER IN
THE NIMAN DANCE AND AS A
RESULT IS OFTEN CALLED THE NIMAN.

Hemis

Aholi

THE UNUSUAL HIGH CONICAL MASK
OF THE AHOLI KACHINA FEATURES
TUFTS OF HAIR IN PLACE OF TAB
EARS. THE AHOLI WEARS A FOX
SKIN RUFF, WHITE KILT, SASH
AND A BLANKET OVER HIS
SHOULDERS THAT IS PAINTED
WITH A LIKENESS OF THE GERM
GOD. THE UPPER PORTION OF THE
BODY IS PAINTED A RED-BROWN
AND IS INTERRUPTED BY A
RECTANGULAR FIELD OF BLUE
OVER THE LEFT SHOULDER AND
YELLOW OVER THE RIGHT. THE
AHOLI CARRIES A STAFF WHICH
IS TOPPED WITH FEATHERS.

THE AHOLI KACHINA APPEARS IN
THE BEAN DANCE AND IS OFTEN
COMPANION OF EOTOTO.

Aholi

Early Morning

THE GREEN CASE MASK OF THE EARLY
MORNING KACHINA HAS SLOT EYES
AND CLOUD SYMBOLS PAINTED ON
THE CHEEKS. LARGE RED EAR TABS
PROJECT FROM THE SIDES OF THE
MASK AND A RED SNOUT FROM
THE FRONT. THE EARLY MORNING
WEARS A WHITE ROBE, THAT IS
INTERRUPTED BY BOLD STRIPES
OF RED, A WHITE KILT AND SASH.
THE BODY IS PAINTED RED AND
YELLOW.

THE EARLY MORNING KACHINA
APPEARS ON HOUSE TOPS AT DAWN
TO SING CRITICAL OR HAPPY SONGS.

Early Morning

Sun

THE MOST STRIKING FEATURE OF THE
SUN KACHINA IS HIS CIRCULAR
MASK THAT IS COMPLETELY SUR-
ROUNDED BY RADIATING EAGLE
FEATHERS. THE CIRCULAR FACE
HAS A RED AND YELLOW FOREHEAD
WHILE THE LOWER HALF IS BLUE.
THE RED BODY IS INTERRUPTED
BY A PATCH OF BLUE OVER THE
RIGHT SHOULDER AND YELLOW
OVER THE LEFT. THE FOREARMS
ARE YELLOW AND THE LOWER LEGS
ARE PAINTED WITH STRIPES OF
YELLOW, RED, BLUE AND BLACK.
THE SUN CARRIES A RATTLE AND
FLUTE.

THE SUN KACHINA REPRESENTS THE
SPIRIT OF THE SUN GOD AND APPEARS
IN MOST OF THE KACHINA DANCES.

The Sun

Bean Dance

THE MASK OF THE BEAN DANCE
KACHINA IS PAINTED GREEN AND
HAS BLACK SLOT EYES. CARVED
WOODEN FLOWERS ARE WORN IN
THE BLACK HAIR. THE UPPER BODY
IS PAINTED BLACK WITH A PATCH
OF GREEN OVER ONE SHOULDER
AND YELLOW OVER THE OTHER. ONE
FOREARM IS PAINTED GREEN WHILE
THE OTHER ONE IS YELLOW. A SASH
IS WORN WITH THE WHITE KILT.
THE BEAN DANCE CARRIES A FLUTE
AND RATTLE.

THE BEAN DANCE KACHINA OFTEN
APPEARS IN GROUPS AND IS THE
MOST IMPORTANT PERFORMER
IN THE BEAN DANCE CEREMONY.

Bean Dance

Chakwaina

THE BLACK SACK STYLE MASK OF
THE CHAKWAINA KACHINA IS
INTERRUPTED BY A CROOKED
WHITE LINE AND FEATURES YELLOW
HALF MOON SHAPED EYES. THE
UPPER BODY IS PAINTED RED WITH
YELLOW SHOULDERS AND FOREARMS.
THE WHITE KILT IS SOMETIMES
MADE OF BUCKSKIN AND A
WOOL SASH IS WORN WITH IT. THE
CHAKWAINA CARRIES A RATTLE
AND BOW.

THE COLORFUL CHAKWAINA IS
SEEN IN THE PAMUYA AT THE
FIRST MESA.

Chakwaina

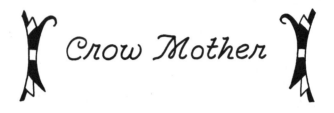

Crow Mother

THE CROW MOTHER KACHINA FEATURES
A BLUE, CASE TYPE MASK WITH
BLACK WINGS ON THE SIDES. THE
FRONT OF THE BLUE MASK IS
INTERRUPTED BY A FIELD OF
BLACK THAT IS OUTLINED IN
WHITE. THE LOWER DRESS IS
BLACK WITH RED AND GREEN
STRIPES. THE WHITE CEREMONIAL
ROBE IS BORDERED WITH GREEN
DESIGNS. THE BOOT MOCCASINS
ARE BLUE WITH RED AND YELLOW
DESIGNS.

THE CROW MOTHER KACHINA IS
MOTHER OF THE HU KACHINA AND
APPEARS IN THE BEAN DANCE.

Crow Mother

Horned Owl

THE UNUSUAL CASE MASK OF THE
HORNED OWL FEATURES STARTLING
YELLOW AND BLACK EYES AND
A PROJECTING BLACK BEAK. A
BUCKSKIN CAPE IS WORN OVER
THE WHITE SHOULDERS AND A
SASH HANGS FROM THE WAIST.
FITTED CLOTH TROUSERS COVER
THE LOWER BODY. THE HORNED
OWL CARRIES A BOW AND A
YUCCA WHIP.

THE HORNED OWL APPEARS IN
MOST KACHINA DANCES TO SPY
ON THE CLOWNS. HE ALSO TAKES
PART IN THE BEAN DANCE AND
THE WATER SERPENT CEREMONY.

Horned Owl

 # Mudhead

THE REDDISH-BROWN COLORED
MASK OF THE MUDHEAD FEATURES
THREE GOURD SHAPED PIECES
PROJECTING FROM THE TOP AND
SIDES. THE ROUND EYES AND
SNOUT PROJECT FROM THE FRONT.
THE MUDHEAD WEARS A BLACK
KILT THAT IS USUALLY MADE
FROM A WOMAN'S OLD DRESS. THE
KILT IS HELD IN PLACE BY A
WIDE LEATHER BELT. THE COMIC
MUDHEAD CARRIES A RATTLE.

THE COMICAL LOOKING MUDHEAD
IS THE MOST COMMON HOPI CLOWN
AND APPEARS IN MIXED KACHINA
DANCES. THE MUDHEAD OFFERS
COMIC RELIEF IN SERIOUS RITES.

Mudhead

 # Ho-o-te

THE BLACK MASK OF THE HO-O-TE
KACHINA FEATURES LARGE CURVING
GREEN AND WHITE HORNS, POP
EYES AND A PROJECTING SNOUT.
THE BODY OF THIS HORNED DOLL
IS PAINTED BLACK WITH YELLOW
SHOULDERS AND FOREARMS. THE
HO-O-TE WEARS THE USUAL
WHITE KACHINA KILT AND WOOL
SASH. HE CARRIES A RATTLE
AND BOW.

THE HO-O-TE KACHINA APPEARS
IN MIXED KACHINA DANCES.

Ho-o-te

Zuni Maiden

THE CASE MASK OF THE ZUNI
MAIDEN IS PAINTED BLACK
WITH WHITE EYES AND FEATURES
ZIGZAG WHITE LINES PAINTED
IN THE CENTER TO REPRESENT A
NOSE. THE ZUNI MAIDEN WEARS
A BLACK WOMAN'S DRESS AND
A WHITE MAIDEN'S SHAWL. THIS
KACHINA IS USUALLY BAREFOOT
AND CARRIES NO REGULAR
ACCESSORIES.

THE ZUNI KACHINA MAIDEN
ACCOMPANIES THE SIO HEMIS
KACHINA AND IN JULY THE
HOPI HEMIS KACHINA IN THE
NIMAN DANCE.

Zuni Maiden

Zuni Rain Priest

THE WHITE CASE MASK OF THE ZUNI
RAIN PRIEST FEATURES A LARGE
HORN PROJECTING FROM ONE
SIDE AND A SMALL EAR TAB FROM
THE OTHER. THE TRIANGULAR
MOUTH AND RECTANGULAR BLACK
EYES ARE PAINTED ON. HE WEARS
A BLACK AND WHITE RUFF, A
WHITE ROBE AND RED MOCCASINS.
THE BODY IS PAINTED WHITE. HE
CARRIES A BOW.

THE ZUNI RAIN PRIEST APPEARS
IN THE BEAN DANCE CEREMONY.

Zuni Rain Priest

Silent

THE GREEN CASE MASK OF THE
SILENT KACHINA HAS DIAGONAL
DESIGNS PAINTED ON THE CHEEKS
AND A PAINTED TRIANGULAR
MOUTH. LARGE TAB EARS PROJECT
FROM THE SIDES OF THE MASK.
THE SILENT KACHINA WEARS A
COLORFUL MAIDEN'S SHAWL,
KILT AND WOMAN'S BELT.

THE SILENT KACHINA APPEARS
IN THE WATER SERPENT DANCE
AND THE BEAN DANCE. HE IS
SAID TO BE THE KACHINA OF THE
PREHISTORIC LADDER DANCE.

Silent

Mong

THE CIRCULAR MASK OF THE MONG
KACHINA IS USUALLY PAINTED HALF
YELLOW AND HALF GREEN WITH
BLACK STARS ON THE YELLOW AND
YELLOW CIRCLES ON THE GREEN.
THE UNUSUAL MASK ALSO HAS A
BLACK CENTRAL AREA FROM
WHICH A BEAK PROJECTS. THE
MONG WEARS A KILT, SASH AND
A WOMAN'S BELT. HE SOMETIMES
CARRIES A GOURD AND WAND.

THE MONG KACHINA, ALSO KNOWN
AS THE GERM GOD OR AHOLA,
APPEARS AT THE BEAN DANCE
TO REPRESENT THE SPIRIT OF
THE GERM GOD WHO CONTROLS
THE GROWTH AND REPRODUCTION
OF ALL THINGS.

Mong

Maiden

THE KACHINA MAIDEN WEARS A YELLOW HALF MASK THAT IS INTERRUPTED BY COLORFUL PARALLEL LINES ACROSS THE LOWER PORTION. THE BLACK HAIR IS ARRANGED IN LARGE MAIDEN'S WHORLS. A WHITE MAIDEN'S SHAWL IS WORN OVER THE SHOULDERS AND BRILLIANT WHITE BOOTS PROJECT FROM BENEATH THE BLACK WOMAN'S DRESS. THE KACHINA MAIDEN OFTEN CARRIES A MUSICAL INSTRUMENT.

THIS MOST COMMON OF KACHINA MAIDENS ACCOMPANIES THE HEMIS KACHINA AS WELL AS MANY OTHER KACHINA PERFORMERS.

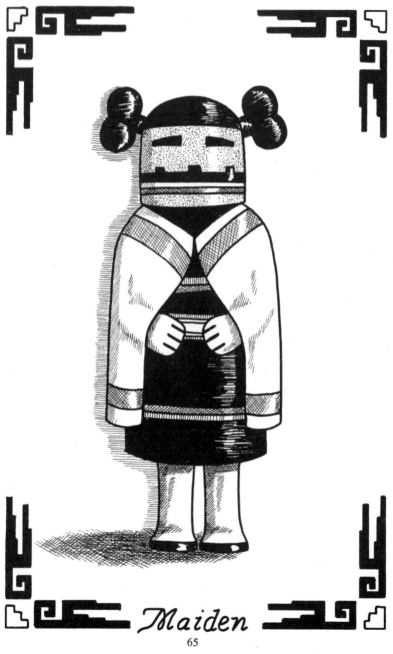

Maiden

Koshare

THE FACE MASK OF THE KOSHARE
IS PAINTED WHITE WITH A BLACK
MOUTH AND EYES. PROJECTING
FROM THE TOP OF HIS HEAD ARE
TWO SOFT BLACK AND WHITE
STRIPED HORNS. THE BLACK AND
WHITE BODY IS COVERED ONLY
BY A BLACK BREECH CLOUT.
THE KOSHARE CARRIES NO
REGULAR ACCESSORIES.

THE KOSHARE, ALSO KNOWN AS
THE HANO CLOWN, APPEARS TO
CONTRIBUTE COMEDY INTERLUDES
TO SOLEMN RELIGIOUS DRAMAS.

Koshare

Snow

THE BLUE CASE MASK OF THE SNOW
KACHINA FEATURES LARGE TAB
EARS AND BLACK SLOT EYES
WHICH ARE PAINTED ON A FIELD OF
WHITE. THE MOUTH IS ALSO PAINTED
ON. HE WEARS A WHITE KILT, FOX
SKIN AND GREEN MOCCASINS.
THE BODY IS PAINTED RED AND
INTERRUPTED BY A FIELD OF
YELLOW WHICH COVERS THE
SHOULDERS AND CHEST. THE
SNOW KACHINA CARRIES A
RATTLE AND FLUTE.

THE SNOW KACHINA APPEARS
IN THE BEAN DANCE, WATER
SERPENT CEREMONY AND IN
SOME MIXED KACHINA DANCES.

Snow

Soyal

THE GREEN CASE MASK OF THE
SOYAL KACHINA HAS PAINTED
SLOT EYES AND A TRIANGULAR
MOUTH. THE MASK HAS NO EARS.
HE WEARS A WHITE SHIRT MADE
OF COTTON CLOTH, A WHITE KILT
AND RED MOCCASINS. THE SOYAL
OFTEN CARRIES A RATTLE AND
BOW.

THE SOYAL KACHINA IS THE FIRST
KACHINA TO APPEAR AT THE
TIME OF THE WINTER SOLSTICE.
IT IS BELIEVED THAT THIS
KACHINA TAUGHT THE HOPI TO
MAKE PRAYER OFFERINGS KNOWN
AS PAHOS.

Soyal

Zuni Warrior

THE CASE MASK OF THE ZUNI
WARRIOR KACHINA MAY BE
PAINTED ANY ONE OF THE SIX
DIRECTIONAL COLORS. THE MASK
FEATURES PAINTED ON FLOWER
EARS, TUBE SHAPED MOUTH
AND EYES THAT ARE JOINED
TOGETHER BY A FIELD OF
WHITE. THE ZUNI WARRIOR
WEARS A WHITE KILT, FOX
SKIN, SASH AND IS USUALLY
BAREFOOT. HE CARRIES YUCCA
LEAF WHIPS.

THE ZUNI WARRIOR KACHINA
APPEARS IN THE BEAN DANCE.

Zuni Warrior

Qoqlo

THE BLACK CASE MASK OF QOQLO
FEATURES WHITE MARKINGS WHICH
REPRESENT BIRD TRACKS. THE
FEATHERS ATTACHED TO THE TOP
AND SIDES OF THE MASK ARE
FROM ALL KINDS OF BIRDS. THE
OUTSTANDING FEATURE OF
THIS KACHINA IS HIS WHITE
MAN'S SUIT OF COAT AND PANTS.
QOQLO CARRIES A RATTLE.

THE STRANGE LOOKING QOQLO
IS A GENEROUS AND KINDLY
KACHINA WHO APPEARS FOUR
NIGHTS BEFORE THE BEAN
DANCE TO PROMISE GOOD CROPS
AND TOYS FOR THE CHILDREN.

Qoqlo

He-e-e

THE FACE MASK OF THE HE-E-E
KACHINA IS PAINTED BLACK
AND FEATURES YELLOW EYES,
A BEARD AND A MAIDEN WHORL
ON ONE SIDE. THE HE-E-E WEARS
A WOMAN'S BLACK DRESS, A
SHAWL, WEDDING SASH AND
RED MOCCASINS. HE CARRIES
A BOW AND RATTLE.

THE HE-E-E KACHINA IS BELIEVED
TO BE THE SPIRIT OF A YOUNG
MAN WHO RALLIED DEFENDERS
OF HIS VILLAGE TO DEFEAT THE
APPROACHING ENEMY.

He-e-e

Mountain Goat

THE CASE MASK OF THE MOUNTAIN
GOAT KACHINA IS PAINTED
WHITE WITH A BLUE FACE WHICH
IS OUTLINED IN RED AND BLACK.
THE COLORFUL MASK FEATURES
CURVED HORNS, A PROJECTING
BLACK SNOUT AND BLOSSOM
EARS. THE BODY IS PAINTED A
LIGHT BLUE AND HE WEARS
A SASH AND WHITE KILT. THE
MOUNTAIN GOAT KACHINA LEANS
ON A CANE.

THE MOUNTAIN GOAT KACHINA
APPEARS IN BANDS AT ORDINARY
KACHINA DANCES AND IS BELIEVED
TO HAVE POWER OVER RAIN.

Mountain Goat

Buffalo

THE FACE MASK OF THE BUFFALO
KACHINA IS PAINTED GREEN AND
FEATURES CURVING HORNS,
ROUND PROJECTING EYES AND
A SNOUT. THE BUFFALO KACHINA
IS SHOWN WEARING A WHITE
KILT, COLORFUL WEDDING SASH
AND WHITE MOCCASINS. HE
CARRIES A RATTLE AND BOW.

THE BUFFALO KACHINA APPEARS
IN ORDINARY KACHINA DANCES.

Buffalo

Navajo Maiden

THE FACE MASK OF THE NAVAJO
KACHINA MAIDEN IS PAINTED
GREEN WITH RED AND YELLOW
PATCHES UNDER THE SLOT
EYES. THE NAVAJO MAIDEN
WEARS THE FAMILIAR NAVAJO
STYLE BLOUSE AND COLORFUL
SKIRT. SHE CARRIES A SPRIG
OF GREEN IN EACH HAND.

THE NAVAJO KACHINA MAIDEN
ACCOMPANIES QOIA.

Navajo Maiden

Yucca

THE GREEN CASE MASK OF THE
YUCCA KACHINA FEATURES SLOT
EYES, SNOUT AND SPOTS UNDER
EACH EYE WHICH REPRESENT
ANIMAL FOOTPRINTS. ON TOP
OF THE MASK IS A TRIPOD
SHAPED HEADDRESS WHICH IS
TRIMMED WITH FEATHERS. THE
YUCCA WEARS A KILT HUNG
WITH YUCCA LEAVES, A FOX
SKIN AND RED MOCCASINS. HE
CARRIES A RATTLE AND BOW.

Yucca

Turquoise Nose Plug

THE BROWN CASE MASK OF THE
TURQUOISE NOSE PLUG KACHINA
FEATURES LARGE EAR TABS,
PROJECTING TUBE SHAPED
MOUTH AND RED HAIR. HIS
BODY IS PAINTED WHITE WITH
BLACK STRIPES AND HE WEARS
A BUCKSKIN PIECE DRAPED
OVER ONE SHOULDER. THE
TURQUOISE NOSE PLUG CARRIES
A YUCCA LEAF WHIP AND BOW.

THE TURQUOISE NOSE PLUG
KACHINA APPEARS IN PAIRS
WITH THE CLOWNS.

Turquoise Nose Plug

Hochani

THE GREEN CASE MASK OF THE
HOCHANI KACHINA FEATURES
A BLACK BAND PAINTED ACROSS
THE EYES AND LARGE EAR TABS
PROJECTING FROM THE SIDES.
THE BODY IS PAINTED RED AND
HE WEARS A WHITE KILT, SASH,
FOX SKIN AND RED MOCCASINS.
HOCHANI OFTEN CARRIES A
RATTLE AND BOW.

THE HOCHANI KACHINA APPEARS
IN MIXED KACHINA DANCES.

Hochani

Tungwup Whipper

THE BLACK CASE MASK OF THE
TUNGWUP WHIPPER FEATURES
WHITE SPOTS ON THE CHEEKS, A
LONG BEARD AND CURVING HORNS.
HE WEARS A WHITE KILT, SASH
AND RED MOCCASINS. THE
TUNGWUP CARRIES YUCCA
LEAF WHIPS AND SOMETIMES
PIECES OF CHOLLA CACTUS.

THE TUNGWUP WHIPPER KACHINA
APPEARS AT THE BEAN DANCE
WITH THE CROW MOTHER.

Tungwup Whipper

Polik Mana

THE POLIK MANA OR BUTTERFLY
KACHINA MAIDEN FEATURES AN
ELABORATE TABLETA AND A
WHITE FACE MASK. THE FACE MASK
HAS PAINTED TRIANGULAR
HACHURED AREAS ON THE CHEEKS
AND THE CHIN AREA IS PAINTED
WITH COLORFUL LINES THAT
RADIATE FROM THE NOSE. THE
POLIK MANA WEARS A WHITE
EMBROIDERED CEREMONIAL
ROBE AND A KILT THAT IS
WORN LIKE A BLOUSE. THE BARE
FEET ARE PAINTED YELLOW.
POLIK MANA CARRIES A FEATHER
IN EACH HAND.

Polik Mana

Pachavu Hu

THE BLACK CASE MASK OF THE
PACHAVU HU KACHINA
FEATURES WHITE SPOTS UNDER
THE EYES, A CROSS-HATCHING
DESIGN ON THE LEFT SIDE OF
THE FOREHEAD AND CURVED
HORNS. THE PACHAVU HU WEARS
A WHITE KILT, SASH AND FOX
SKIN. HIS BODY IS PAINTED
WHITE AND HE CARRIES A
YUCCA LEAF WHIP IN EACH
HAND.

THE PACHAVU HU KACHINA,
ALSO KNOWN AS THE PACHAVU
WHIPPER, APPEARS ONLY AT
THE BEAN DANCE IN THE
INITIATION YEARS.

94

Pachavu Hu

Crow Bride

THE GREEN CASE MASK OF THE
CROW BRIDE IS SIMILAR IN
EVERY WAY TO THAT OF THE CROW
MOTHER KACHINA. THE CROW
BRIDE WEARS A WEDDING
DRESS AND CEREMONIAL ROBE.
SHE CARRIES A PLAQUE WITH
CORN MEAL.

THERE IS CONFUSION IN REGARD
TO THE CROW MOTHER AND BRIDE
KACHINAS. SOME HOPI BELIEVE
THEM TO BE SEPARATE KACHINAS,
WHILE OTHERS CONSIDER THEM
TO BE ONE AND THE SAME.

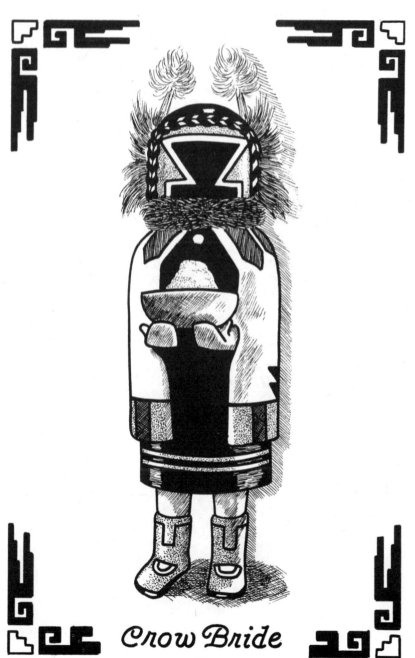

Crow Bride

Kokopolo

THE CASE MASK OF THE KOKOPOLO
KACHINA FEATURES A LINE MADE
OF FELT RUNNING VERTICALLY
FROM THE TURNED-UP BEAK UP
OVER THE TOP OF THE HEAD. HE
WEARS A WHITE SHIRT WITH
ORANGE STITCHES AND A WHITE
KILT. KOKOPOLO CARRIES A
LONG STICK AND A RATTLE.

THE KOKOPOLO APPEARS IN
MIXED KACHINA DANCES. HE IS
IDENTIFIED WITH THE HUMPED-
BACK FLUTE PLAYER WHEN HE
BORROWS A FLUTE FROM THE
FLUTE KACHINA.

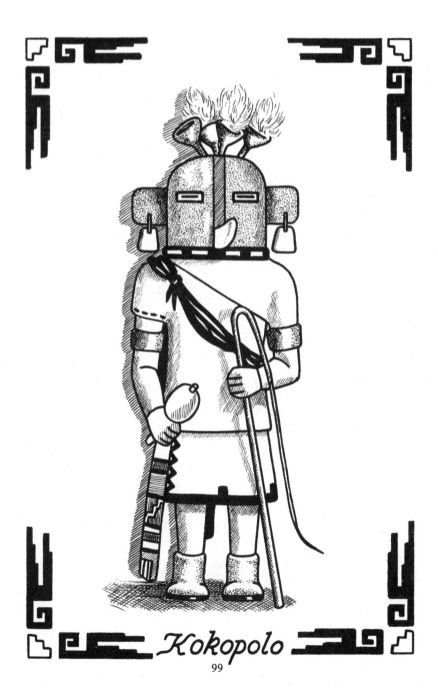

Kokopolo

Star

THE GREEN CASE MASK OF THE
STAR KACHINA FEATURES A
FOUR POINTED BLACK STAR
PAINTED ON THE FACE. LARGE
EAGLE FEATHERS RADIATE
FROM THE BACK OF THE MASK
AND BLACK YARN HANGS AT
THE SIDES. STAR WEARS A
FUR RUFF AND YELLOW KILT
WHICH HAS A WIDE BROWN
BORDER. THE BODY OF THE
STAR KACHINA IS PAINTED
EITHER RED OR BLACK WITH
YELLOW SHOULDERS AND
FOREARMS. HE CARRIES A
YUCCA LEAF WHIP IN EACH
HAND.

Star
101

Left-handed

THE BLACK CASE MASK OF THE
LEFT-HANDED KACHINA FEATURES
DIAMOND SHAPED EYES, A BEARD
AND PROJECTING EAR TABS. HE
WEARS A BREECH CLOUT AND
A SHEEP OR ANTELOPE SKIN
DRAPED FROM ONE SHOULDER.
THE RIGHT ARM AND LEG ARE
PRINTED WITH HORIZONTAL WHITE
STRIPES. THE BODY AND LEFT
ARM AND LEG ARE BLACK. THE
LEFT-HANDED KACHINA OFTEN
CARRIES A BOW IN HIS RIGHT
HAND.

THE LEFT-HANDED KACHINA IS
SEEN IN MIXED DANCES AND
SEPARATELY AS A WARRIOR.

Left-handed

Mocking

THE BROWN CASE MASK OF THE
MOCKING KACHINA FEATURES
JUNIPER BARK HAIR AND LONG
TUBULAR EYES AND MOUTH. THE
THREE WHITE LINES PAINTED UNDER
THE EYES ARE SYMBOLS. HE
WEARS A BLACK AND WHITE RUFF,
AN OLD SHIRT AND BREECH CLOUT.
THE MOCKING KACHINA CARRIES A
RATTLE AND LONG CANE.

THE MOCKING KACHINA APPEARS
IN MIXED DANCES AND IS NOTED
FOR MAKING FUN OF EVERYONE.

Mocking

Compassion

THE GREEN CASE MASK OF THE
COMPASSION KACHINA FEATURES
SLOT EYES, PROJECTING TAB
EARS, A PAINTED TRIANGULAR
MOUTH AND BLACK HACHURE
DESIGNS ON THE CHEEKS. THE
BODY IS PAINTED RED WITH
ONE YELLOW AND ONE GREEN
SHOULDER. HE WEARS A FOX
SKIN RUFF, WHITE KILT AND
COLORFUL SASH. COMPASSION
CARRIES A RATTLE AND MANO.

THE COMPASSION KACHINA IS
SEEN AT THE BEAN DANCE AND
SYMPATHIZES WITH CHILDREN
WHO ARE ABOUT TO BE PUNISHED.

Compassion

Marao

THE CASE MASK OF THE MARAO
KACHINA MAY BE PAINTED IN
A VARIETY OF WAYS, BUT IT
ALWAYS FEATURES A SNOUT
WITH TEETH, BLOSSOM TYPE
EARS AND A TRIPOD SHAPED
HEADDRESS. HE WEARS A FIR
RUFF, KILT, SASH AND FOX
SKIN. HIS BODY IS OFTEN
PAINTED WHITE.

THE MARAO KACHINA IS SAID
TO BE A ZUNI TYPE AND IS
ALSO QUITE VARIABLE. HE IS
SEEN IN REGULAR DANCES.

Marao

Black Ogre

THE CASE MASK OF THE BLACK
OGRE KACHINA IS PAINTED
BLACK AND FEATURES A LARGE
TOOTHED SNOUT AND SIDE HORNS.
HE WEARS A BUCKSKIN SHIRT,
FORM-FITTING TROUSERS, RED
LEGGINGS AND COLORFUL SASH.
THE BLACK OGRE CARRIES A BOW.

THE BLACK OGRE KACHINA, ALSO
KNOWN AS NATA-ASKA, IS SAID
TO ACCOMPANY THE SOYOKO
KACHINA TO COLLECT FOOD FROM
THE HOPI CHILDREN.

Black Ogre

Spotted Corn

THE RED CASE MASK OF THE ZUNI
TYPE SPOTTED CORN KACHINA
FEATURES A TUBE SNOUT, TAB
EARS AND POT HOOK SHAPED EYES.
THE EYES ARE SURROUNDED BY
A TERRACED AREA OF WHITE.
FOUR FEATHERS FORM A HORI-
ZONTAL CROSS ON THE TOP OF
THE MASK. THE BODY IS PAINTED
PINK OR RED WITH WHITE CIRCLES.
HE WEARS A BLACK BREECH CLOUT,
SASH AND RED MOCCASINS.

THE SPOTTED CORN, OR AVACHHOYA
KACHINA, APPEARS IN REGULAR
KACHINA DANCES.

Spotted Corn

Fire God

THE CASE MASK OF THE ZUNI
FIRE GOD IS PAINTED BLACK
WITH SPOTS OF ALL COLORS.
THE MASK OFTEN FEATURES
A TUBE MOUTH. THE BODY OF
THE BAREFOOT FIRE GOD IS
PAINTED BLACK WITH SPOTS
OF ALL COLORS. HE SOMETIMES
CARRIES A BOW AND ARROWS.

THE ZUNI FIRE GOD APPEARS
IN THE PAMUYA.

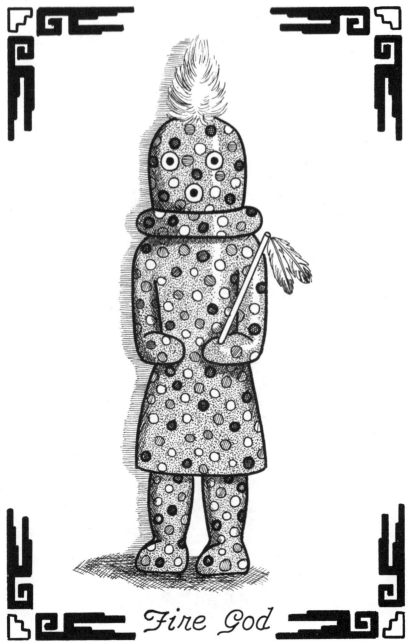

Fire God

Mastof

THE UNUSUAL BLACK CASE MASK
OF THE MASTOF KACHINA IS
PAINTED WITH WHITE DOTS ON
THE FACE WHICH REPRESENT
CONSTELLATIONS. A GRASS
RUFF SEPARATES THE MASK
FROM THE BLACK BODY AND
THE KILT IS MADE FROM A
WOMAN'S DISCARDED DRESS.
THE MASTOF KACHINA CARRIES
A RATTLE AND THROWING STICK.

THE MASTOF KACHINA IS SAID
TO REPRESENT THE SPIRIT OF
THE EARTH GOD AND APPEARS
IN INITIATION YEARS AT THE
SOLSTICE CEREMONY.

Mastof

Salako Maiden

THE ELABORATE TABLETA OF
THE SALAKO MAIDEN KACHINA
IS OFTEN PAINTED WITH CLOUD
SYMBOLS. THE WHITE FACE
MASK FEATURES THE CHIN
SECTION PAINTED ALL COLORS
WHICH RADIATE FROM THE
NOSE. THE BODY IS COVERED
WITH EAGLE FEATHERS AND
A WEDDING ROBE IS WORN
OVER THE SHOULDERS.

THE SALAKO MAIDEN KACHINA
APPEARS AT THE SALAKO
CEREMONY, WHICH IS RARELY
GIVEN.

Salako Maiden

Heheya

THE CASE MASK OF THE HEHEYA
IS PAINTED GREEN OR YELLOW
WITH VERTICAL ZIGZAG LINES
ON THE FACE. THE NOSE IS
REPRESENTED BY A PAINTED
"T" SHAPED DESIGN. TAB EARS
PROJECT FROM THE SIDES OF
THE MASK. THE HEHEYA WEARS
A ROBE WHICH COVERS MOST
OF HIS RED AND YELLOW BODY.
HE USUALLY CARRIES A RATTLE.

THE HEHEYA KACHINA APPEARS
IN PAIRS WITH THE OGRES AND
SOYOKO.

Heheya

Wolf

THE CASE MASK OF THE MODERN
ACTION TYPE WOLF KACHINA IS
PAINTED BROWN AND FEATURES
ANIMAL EARS AND SNOUT WITH
LARGE FANGS. THE BODY IS
PAINTED BROWN AND HE WEARS
A BLACK BREECH CLOUT. THE
FOREARMS AND LOWER LEGS
ARE PAINTED BLACK WITH WHITE
SPOTS. THE WOLF KACHINA LEANS
ON A CANE.

THE WOLF KACHINA APPEARS
IN THE WATER SERPENT CEREMONY
AND MIXED KACHINA DANCES.

The Wolf

Spotted Corn

THE WHITE MASK OF THE ACTION
TYPE SPOTTED CORN KACHINA
FEATURES TAB EARS, PROJECTING
TUBE MOUTH AND FOUR FEATHERS
WHICH FORM A HORIZONTAL CROSS
ON THE TOP. THE BODY IS PAINTED
BLACK AND WHITE WITH BROWN
STRIPES RUNNING DOWN THE
OUTSIDE OF EACH LEG. THE
SPOTTED CORN WEARS A BLACK
BREECH CLOUT AND COLORFUL
SASH. PIECES OF WOOL YARN
ARE TIED AT BOTH WRISTS AND
BELOW EACH KNEE.

SPOTTED CORN IS THE YOUNGER
BROTHER OF THE HEMIS AND
APPEARS IN REGULAR DANCES.

Spotted Corn

Visiting The Hopi

THE HOPI INDIANS ARE FRIENDLY
AND HOSPITABLE AND TOURISTS ARE
WELCOME TO ATTEND THEIR
CEREMONIES. THE VISITOR
SHOULD REMEMBER THAT HE
IS A GUEST AND APPROPRIATE
BEHAVIOR IS EXPECTED. BE AS
UNOBTRUSIVE AS POSSIBLE AND
IN NO WAY INTERFERE OR
INTERRUPT ANY CEREMONY.
TAKING PHOTOGRAPHS OR
SKETCHING PICTURES DURING
A RELIGIOUS CEREMONY IS
ABSOLUTELY FORBIDDEN. ANY
RECORDING EQUIPMENT, SKETCH
PADS OR CAMERAS USED IN
VIOLATION OF THESE RULES
WILL BE CONFISCATED BY
VILLAGE AUTHORITIES.

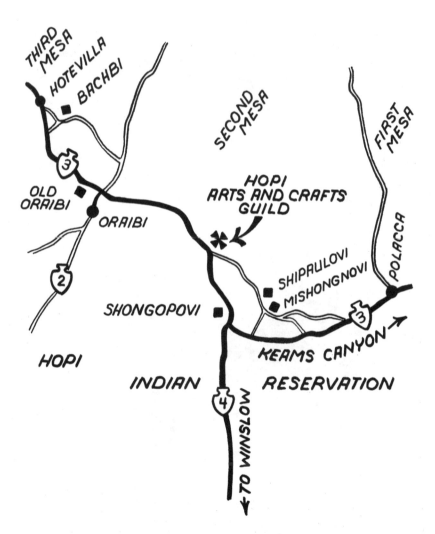

THE HOPI VILLAGES CAN EASILY BE
REACHED BY TRAVELING U.S. ROUTE 89
NORTH FROM FLAGSTAFF TO TUBA
CITY. AT TUBA CITY TAKE RESERVATION
HIGHWAY 3 EAST. TO HOTEVILLA.